COLIN POWELL

A Little Golden Book® Biography

By Frank Berrios
Illustrated by Kristin Sorra

A GOLDEN BOOK • NEW YORK

Text copyright © 2024 by Frank Berrios
Cover art and interior illustrations copyright © 2024 by Kristin Sorra
All rights reserved. Published in the United States by Golden Books, an imprint of
Random House Children's Books, a division of Penguin Random House LLC, 1745 Broadway,
New York, NY 10019. Golden Books, A Golden Book, A Little Golden Book, the G colophon,
and the distinctive gold spine are registered trademarks of Penguin Random House LLC.
rhcbooks.com
Educators and librarians, for a variety of teaching tools, visit us at RHTeachersLibrarians.com
Library of Congress Control Number: 2022941218
ISBN 978-0-593-64504-8 (trade) — ISBN 978-0-593-64505-5 (ebook)
Printed in the United States of America
10 9 8 7 6 5 4 3 2 1

CANDY · SODA · SNACKS
GROCERY · COFFEE · BAKERY
DELI · MAGAZINES · COMICS

Colin Luther Powell was born on April 5, 1937, in Harlem, New York. His parents, Luther and Maud Ariel Powell, were immigrants from Jamaica.

His father worked for a company that made women's clothes and his mother worked as a seamstress. Colin also had an older sister named Marilyn. Their parents wanted them both to work hard and get a good education.

When Colin was young, his family moved to an apartment in the South Bronx. The diverse neighborhood had Puerto Rican grocery stores and Jewish bakeries. Black, Irish, and Italian families lived next to each other in crowded apartment buildings.

Colin tried hard at school, but unlike his sister, he didn't always get the best grades. He took flute and piano lessons, but Colin didn't have a passion for music, either.

Instead, Colin enjoyed playing baseball, football, and stickball with his neighborhood friends. They rode bicycles and loved to play checkers.

He also liked to fly kites. Colin and his friends would often pretend their kites were planes, flying missions during a war.

Colin came from a large, loving family. His aunts, uncles, and cousins all lived nearby. Everyone encouraged him to aim for success and dream big.

Colin was also a hard worker. After he helped unload a truck at a local shop, the owner offered him a part-time job. Most of the customers spoke Yiddish, a language spoken by Jewish people. Soon, Colin could speak Yiddish, too—which was very helpful when trying to make sales!

After high school, Colin enrolled at City College of New York. Soon, he joined the Reserve Officers' Training Corps. The ROTC trained and prepared young college students to become officers in the United States Armed Forces.

Colin was filled with pride and purpose from the very first day he put on his ROTC uniform. He had found something he really enjoyed doing!

One summer, Colin got a job at a bottling plant. On his first day he noticed that everyone holding a mop or a broom was Black, while all the other workers were white. This was unfair, but Colin needed the job. He grabbed the mop he was given and worked hard every day.

Colin's supervisor was impressed with his work and asked him to come back the next summer.

"Not behind a mop," replied Colin. Instead, he wanted to work on the bottling machines. That job paid more money. The supervisor agreed. The following year, Colin quickly rose to become the deputy shift leader.

In 1958, Colin graduated from college. As an ROTC graduate, he was now an army officer, eager to begin his new career as a professional soldier in the United States Army.

Several years later, Colin went on a blind date with a woman named Alma Johnson from Birmingham, Alabama. She was smart and sweet. Before long, Colin was in love!

In 1962, Colin and Alma got married in Alma's hometown. They would go on to have three children—Michael, Linda, and Annemarie.

The same year Colin and Alma were married,
Colin received his orders to go to Vietnam,
a country in Southeast Asia that was at war.
   In 1968, Colin broke his ankle in a helicopter
crash. Even though he was injured, he rescued
three men from the wreckage. Colin's bravery
earned him the Soldier's Medal!

Being away from his wife and kids was never easy for Colin. So when he was home, he spent as much time as possible with his family.

Colin would go on to hold many important positions during his thirty-five years in the army. Eventually, he would become a four-star general— the nation's highest military rank.

In 1987, Colin was chosen to be national security advisor to President Ronald Reagan. He was responsible for helping the president keep the country safe. Colin was the first Black man to hold this position.

Under President George H. W. Bush, and again under President Bill Clinton, Colin served as chairman of the Joint Chiefs of Staff.

Later, under President George W. Bush, Colin was appointed as secretary of state. He advised the president on issues that dealt with other countries.

Colin was again the first Black man to hold each of these important positions!

Still, one of the proudest moments of his career was the unveiling ceremony of a statue to honor the Black veterans known as Buffalo Soldiers.

From the start, free and enslaved Black people fought for this country. But the Buffalo Soldiers were the first all-Black troops officially allowed to fight in the military after the Civil War.

During his career, Colin worked with both Republican and Democratic presidents.

First and foremost, he was a proud American who understood the necessity for different styles of leadership. Whenever his country needed him, Colin always answered the call!

After retiring, Colin stayed busy writing books about his life and working with organizations that help young people.

In 2008, Colin surprised many when, as a Republican, he endorsed a Democratic senator, Barack Obama, for president. Colin was inspired by his message of hope and believed Obama was ready for the job. Obama won the election and became the first Black president in US history!

Colin Luther Powell was a young boy from a hardworking family who went on to become one of the top leaders of our nation.

When he passed away on October 18, 2021, former presidents, first ladies, and heads of state from around the world all attended his funeral. His deep love for America and his dedication to service will continue to inspire many for years to come.